ULTIMATE MINECRAFT SECRETS

AN UNOFFICIAL GUIDE TO MINECRAFT TIPS, TRICKS AND HINTS YOU MAY NOT KNOW

BY HEROBRINE BOOKS

Table of Contents

Introduction 1
The Killer Bunny 3
Giant Mobs 4
Turn Your Mobs Upside Down 6
Spawn Zombie Horses 8
Rainbow Sheep 9
A Very Special Bunny 10
Visit The Secret Biome 11
Ocean Monument Riches 12
Lava Waterfall 14
The Best Lawnmower 15
Magic Scissors 16
Flying Cows And Pigs 17
The Power Of Lightning 18
Instant Trash Can 20
Giant Trees 21
Magic Carpet 22
Make A Lava Lamp 23
Quick Equip 24
Shift It All Around 25
I Have A Need For Speed 27
Swimming Up Stream 28
Mob Proofing 29
Quick, Hide! 31
Fire Protection 32
Always Land On Your Feet 33
Never Die 35

Breathe Underwater 36
Gone Fishing 37
Skeletons In The Closet 38
Give That Dog A Skeleton 39
Night Of The Creeps 40
Secret Lives Of Endermen 41
Endermen Stuck At Work 43
Enderbugs, Yuck! 44
Silverfish—Watch Your Feet! 45
Blaze Snowball Fight 46
Put The Zombie Pigmen On A Time Out 47
Clash Of The Titans 49
The Walking Dead...Villager 50
Chicken Jockey 51
My Bodyguard 53
Guardians Of The Ocean Galaxy 54
The Mob Circus 56
Trading Up 57
Man's Best Friend 59
Meow! 60
Colored Baby Sheep 61
Cowboy Pigs 62
The Most Important Meal Of The Day 63
Fill Up Your Saddle Bags 64
Taming And Breeding Magic 65
Remote Control 67
Shoot Fireworks...Sideways! 68
Stained Glass 69
H20 Magic 70
Infinite Water 71
Easier Obsidian 72
Mob Sand 73
Bouncy Blocks 74
Going Sailing? 75

Regular Or Unleaded? 76
What Time Is It? 77
Nuclear Bomb 78
Secret Paintings 79
You Need Your Sleep! 80
Round Trip Teleport 81
Pour That Energy Drink On Your Head 82
Conclusion 83

Introduction

Welcome to Ultimate Minecraft Secrets, Minecraft Tips, Tricks and Hints You May Not Know!

Now, if you've been playing Minecraft for a while then you probably have hundreds of tips and tricks that have allowed you to dominate the game and impress all of your friends. So we know that you are already a Minecraft master and we respect you for that. That is why we did a lot of research for this guide to find all of the new and exciting tricks and tips that will keep you entertained and make you an even better Minecraft pro.

Now, you will probably find tips that you already knew, but I'm sure you will find more that you can add to your collection.

The tips in this book have been tested with the release of 1.8.1 Minecraft update. As the updates continue, we will do our best to continue to add and update all the information in this book.

With that said, let's learn some fun facts about Minecraft!

The Killer Bunny

You can spawn a cute, but killer rabbit by using the following command line:

1. The Killer Rabbit

/summon Rabbit ~ ~ ~ {RabbitType:99}

Hit the rabbit once, and its eyes will glow red as it attacks you! By the way, 2 hits from this killer bunny and you're dead.

Giant Mobs

You can spawn giant versions of different mobs by using the following commands in the command line:

2. Giant Zombie

/summon Giant

3. Giant Wither

/summon WitherBoss ~ ~ ~ {Invul:25000,CustomName:Grumm}

4. Giant Slime

/summon Slime ~ ~ ~ {Size:20}

5. Giant Magma Cube

/summon LavaSlime ~ ~ ~ {Size:20}

Just as a side note, the giant zombie is not very hostile, while the Wither Boss will destroy you!

Turn Your Mobs Upside Down

You can spawn mobs upside down by using the following command in the command line :

6. Upside Down Mob Command

/summon <name of mob here>~ ~ ~ {CustomName:Grumm}. Example: /summon Cow ~ ~ ~ {CustomName:Grumm}

7. Use Nametags

You can also turn mobs upside down by creating a nametag with an Anvil and giving it the name "Dinnerbone" or "Grumm." Any mob that you apply the nametag to will turn upside down.

8. Ride Upside Down

If you turn an animal upside down you can ride, like a horse or pig, you can add a saddle and even ride them upside down!

9. Piggy Nipples

Also, upside down pigs have nipples!

Spawn Zombie Horses

You can spawn zombie horses, or even skeleton horses by using the following commands in the command line:

10. Zombie Horse

/summon EntityHorse ~ ~ ~ {Type:3}

11. Skeleton Horse

/summon EntityHorse ~ ~ ~ {Type:4}

12. Ride Your Own Undead Horse

Just throw a saddle on it and you can ride your own undead horse!

Rainbow Sheep

You can spawn a rainbow sheep by using the following command line.

13. Rainbow Sheep

/summon Sheep ~ ~ ~ {CustomName:jeb_}

14. Use a Nametag

You can also create this effect by creating a name tag with an Anvil, with the name "jeb_". Once you apply the nametag to a sheep it will change colors!

15. Colored Wool? Naw!

Just remember, if you shear it, you will get wool the color of the original sheep.

A Very Special Bunny

16. A Rabbit Named Toast

You can summon a special rabbit named "Toast" by using the command below:

/summon Rabbit ~ ~ ~ {CustomName:Toast}

Visit The Secret Biome

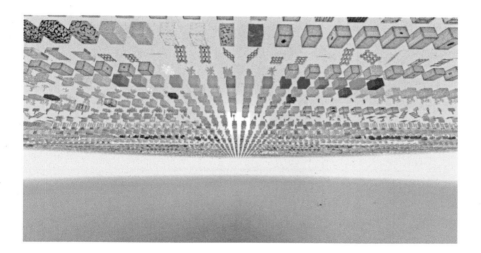

17. The Secret Biome

On the main menu, if you hold down shift while looking at other world options you will get the option to go on Debug mode. Click it and see Minecraft in a whole new way.

Ocean Monument Riches

18. The Ocean Monument

You can visit the ocean monument, which only exists in the deep ocean biome. It contains the following treasures:

19. Gold

The Treasure Chamber of each Ocean Monument contains 8 gold blocks, hidden behind Dark Prismarine.

20. Prismarine

Prismarine itself is only found in Ocean Monuments, so if you want to use it in your own buildings, you have to take it from here.

21. Sea Lanterns

Sea Lanterns are useful light sources for underwater structures. You can collect them using a tool enchanted with Silk Touch, otherwise they will break and you will only get Prismarine Crystals.

22. Prismarine Shards and Prismarine Crystals

These are sometimes dropped by the Guardians when you killed them. These items are used in crafting Sea Lanterns, Prismarine Bricks and Dark Prismarines.

23. Sponges

Sponges can be found in Ocean Monuments, either in rooms where they are attached to the ceiling, or dropped by the Elder Guardian.

Lava Waterfall

24. Lava and Water Waterfall

If you place lava one block above, and three blocks to the left of a water block, you will be able to create a lava waterfall next to a regular waterfall.

The Best Lawnmower

25. The Best Lawnmower

The best lawnmower is a water bucket; it gets rid of cobwebs, grass, flowers and carpets.

Magic Scissors

26. Enchanted Shears

Unlike most tools, shears don't lose durability when breaking blocks they aren't designed to harvest. Since blocks like glowstone, grass blocks, glass, bookshelves, and many others can be harvested without a specific tool, you can use enchanted Silk Touch shears to mine them without losing durability.

Flying Cows And Pigs

27. Flying Cows and Pigs

In creative mode you can attach a lead to an animal and fly with the animal in tow. If you drop them, make sure you're over water.

The Power Of Lightning

28. Summon Lightning

A lightning bolt can be summoned with the command—/summon LightningBolt

29. Charged Creepers

If a lightning hits a creeper, it is going to become charged with an increased explosion power.

30. Charged Pig

If a lightning hits a pig, it's going to turn into a zombie pigman.

31. Charged Villager

If a lightning hits a villager, it's going to turn into a witch.

32. Remote Control Portal

If a lightning hits a nether portal, it will activate it.

33. Remote Control TNT Detonator

If a lightning hits TNT, it will activate it.

34. Destroy and Create

In creative, if you left click and right click in a block at the same time with a block in your hand, it will destroy the block and place the blocks at the same time.

Instant Trash Can

35. All-Natural Trash Can

Throw your garbage away in cactus. This works for all garbage, not just food.

Giant Trees

36. Growing Giant Trees

You can grow a giant spruce tree by placing four spruce saplings down in four blocks of dirt next to each other in a square. Then add bone meal and you'll have a giant spruce tree. You can do this with Jungle trees too.

Magic Carpet

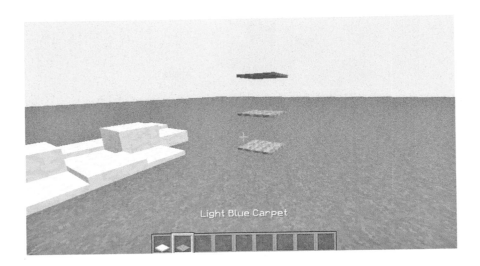

Light Blue Carpet

37. Carpet Tower

Need to get to a high place? You can create a high column of carpets into the air and use water to destroy them and safely come down.

Make A Lava Lamp

38. Make a Lava Lamp

If you want to make an impressive-looking light feature in your base or find yourself running out of torches, you can use lava as a source of light because lava emits the maximum light level of 15 units (Redstone emits 9 units and Torch emits 14 units).

Quick Equip

39. Quick Armor

You can right-click on a piece of armor on the Hot Bar to equip it.

40. Quick Armor On and Off

If you open your inventory you can shift-click your armor on and off.

Shift It All Around

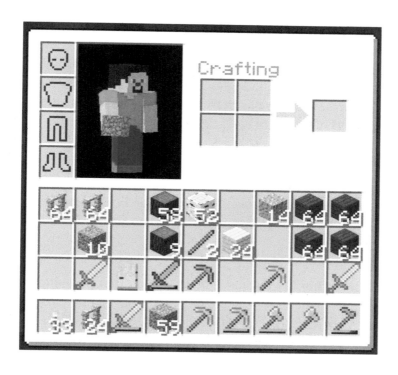

41. Use Hotkeys

In your inventory screen, you can use the hotkey numbers on your keyboard to choose where you want things to go. This also works with items.

42. Drop it All

Hold control and hit the drop key to drop a whole stack of items.

43. Shift Everything Around

Press shift while clicking things in your inventory to shift whole stacks or items around, and you can also use the number keys to shift items into you hotbar.

44. Filler Up!

In your inventory, hold a stack of items or anything more than one. Hold right click on one empty spot in your inventory and move your mouse around, and every empty slot your mouse touches would have one of the item you are holding in it. Do the same thing with left clicking and Minecraft will try as hard as it can to make sure there is the same amounts of that item in all of the slots you touch.

45. Middle Click

Middle clicking items in the world will select the corresponding item in your hot bar. For instance, if you middle click on wood and you have wood in hot bar, then wood will be selected.

46. Transfer All Items

When transferring objects into a chest, if you pick up the item, hover over another of the same item, press shift and double click on that item, it will transfer all of that item into or from your chest.

I Have A Need For Speed

47. Go Faster

If you sprint and jump at the same time it's faster than just sprinting.

48. Just Add Ice

Sprint jumping on ice is faster than just sprint jumping.

49. Trapdoor Anyone?

Sprint jumping on ice on trapdoors under a 2 block high area is one of the fastest ways to travel.

Swimming Up Stream

50. Swimming Up Stream

You swim up water faster if it`s enclosed with blocks or chests.

Mob Proofing

There are many ways to make mob-proof entrances or areas. Here's a few:

51. Carpet On Top Of Fence

Place a carpet on top of a fence post. It allows you to go over the fence, but mobs cannot.

52. Use The Trapdoor

Place a trapdoor on the ground in a 2-block space.

53. Use Slabs

On a vertical 3-block opening, place a slab on top and bottom.

54. Nether/Wood Fence Combo

Create a fence with the entrance as a nether brick fence and wood fence side-by-side. You will be able to fit through, but animals and mobs cannot.

55. Walking Through The Gap

You can destroy the corners of your animal pen, and you can go through the gap, but mobs and animals can't.

56. Carpet Force Field

Dig a long drop and then covered it with signs. Last cover it with carpets and mobs will not dare step on it.

Quick, Hide!

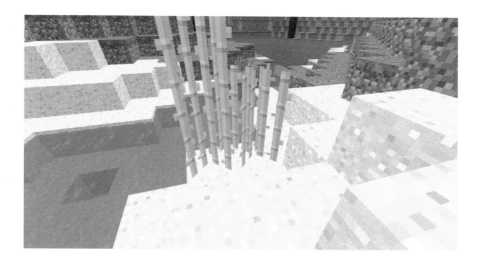

57. Get Ready To Hide

Mobs can't see through vines, sugarcane or too tall grass. So, if all else fails, hide!

Fire Protection

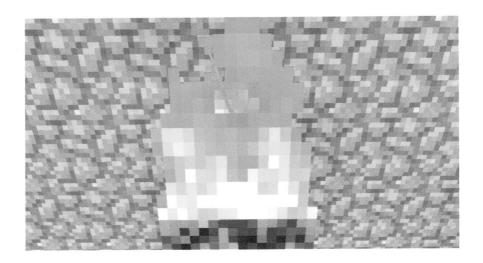

58. Glass Shield

If you put a single block of glass in front of you, it will absorb almost all your damage taken from a TNT explosion.

59. Cobweb Shield

If you stand inside a cobweb near TNT, it will partially block the explosion damage.

60. Block With A Sword

You can block some damage from explosions with a sword.

Always Land On Your Feet

61. Water Bucket

If you're planning to jump from some place high, make sure you have a water bucket in your hand and keep pressing the space bar and you might just survive.

62. Hang Onto That Ladder

If you are falling down from a pillar, place a ladder and catch the side of the ladder (not the top) to break your fall, even one ladder works.

63. Swing On The Vine

A ladder or vines at the end of a fall can save your life. Vines are recommended, because if you land on top of a vine you will not take fall damage.

64. Use A Cobweb Cushion

If you are falling from a high place and you have a cobweb in your hand, you can throw the cobweb out when you are near the ground and use it as an air cushion for landing.

65. Lava Drop

If you have a fire resistance potion a pillar of lava can be used as a quick drop.

66. Fall With a Boat or Minecart

If you fall down while in a boat or a minecart, press left-shift right before you hit the ground, and eject from the boat or minecart, and you will only take damage equal to if you fell at the height of when you left the boat or minecart.

Never Die

67. Make An Easy Exit

If you fall from a really high place and you really don't want to lose all your stuff, get ready to exit out really quick, and then come back into your world again. You could still be falling, but you will safely arrive. You won't take any fall damage, because you just start the world, and it takes about 3 or 4 seconds until you can get started.

Breathe Underwater

68. Breathing Underwater

While in water the following things give a little airpocket: fences, nether fences, iron bars, glass panes, fence gates, trap doors, ladders, slabs, doors, cobblestone walls, sugarcane and signs.

69. Quick Gulp Of Air

If you are underwater and find yourself running out of water, you can hold an empty bucket in your hand, then right-clicking your mouse, it will create a temporary block where you can breathe. But bear in mind that only empty bucket will work, once the bucket is full of water, you have to empty it. This is highly useful when exploring the ocean monument.

Gone Fishing

70. Fish When Its Wet

The best time to go fishing is when it's raining

71. The Big Catch

With two pieces of string, three sticks and roughly 20 minutes, you can obtain precisely 65 fish minus your misses. Cook the salmon and fish, that 5—6 half-a-hunger bars.

Skeletons In The Closet

72. Hide In The Closet

You can avoid skeleton damage by creating a cave one block deep in a stone wall and waiting for the skeleton to come to you. When it gets to the entrance of your mini-cave, it will shoot arrows at you, but they won't do damage. Then you can kill the skeleton with just a few blows.

Give That Dog A Skeleton

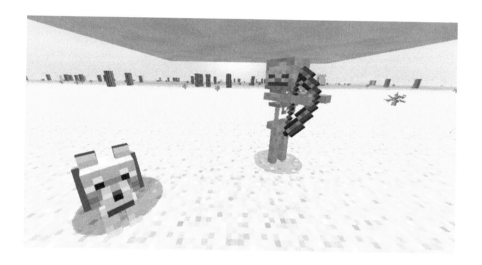

73. Give That Dog A Bone

Skeletons are now afraid of dogs and wolves.

Night Of The Creeps

74. Kill Shot

You can "detonate" a creeper with one hit of flint and steel.

75. Minimal Damage

While on slabs, creepers only blow up the block underneath them.

76. Natural Knockback

You can sprint-hit creepers for natural knockback.

77. Use Your Head

Charged creepers' explosions can cause mob heads to drop, so creating charged creeper farms might be a good idea.

Secret Lives Of Endermen

78. Aim For The Feet

You can kill Endermen easily by hitting them in the feet. Also, hitting the legs of an Enderman won't make it teleport.

79. Be a Master of Disguise

If you have a pumpkin on your head Endermen will not attack you. You can attack them without being attacked in return. Use your F5 feature to see better.

80. Arrow Proof

Endermen you have shot an arrow or any projectile at will teleport away and become hostile. They won't take damage.

81. Through The Looking Glass

You can look at Endermen through glass, and they won't be aggravated toward you.

Endermen Stuck At Work

82. Stuck Enderman

Endermen cannot teleport when they are in Minecarts.

Enderbugs, Yuck!

83. Enderbugs, Run!

Endermites sometimes spawn when a player teleports using an ender pearl.

84. Short Life Span

Endermites despawns after 2 minutes (unless it is named using a name tag).

85. Endermen Lure

Endermites attract Endermen, so you can use them to lure Enderman, making it more easy to collect Ender Pearls.

Silverfish—Watch Your Feet!

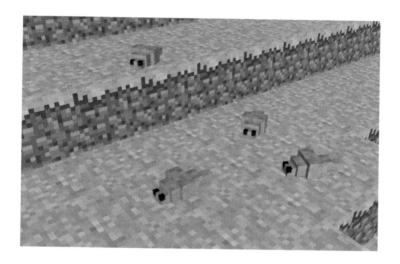

86. Does Anyone Have A Lighter?

If you're going up against silverfish, hit them with a flint and steel lighter so they can't reproduce. Or you can use an enchanted sword to kill with one strike.

87. Re-Appear!

When a silverfish disappears on top of a stone block, break that block and they will appear again.

88. Use The Magic Touch

If you use a Silk touch pick axe on a silverfish block, the silverfish will not spawn.

Blaze Snowball Fight

89. Not A Winter Person

Monsters like the Blaze can be hurt with snowballs.

90. If You Can't See Me, You Can't Hurt Me!

Always make a two block high pillar you can hide behind when you are fighting Blazes.

91. Cobweb Trap

You can trap a Blaze temporarily in cobwebs and if it gets stuck in it, it cannot shoot at you.

Put The Zombie Pigmen On A Time Out

92. Take a Time Out

If you aggravate zombie pigmen, by moving away from their tracking radius (40 blocks away), after 40 seconds, they will calm down.

93. Just One Shot

If you kill a zombie pigman with one hit, the other zombie pigmen will not come after you. You can use an enchanted sword to kill them with one hit.

94. Sword Exchange

You can get gold swords from pigmen by throwing your stone or iron sword into a pit filled with Zombie pigmen. Just, wait a few seconds and go into the pit to pick up your new gold sword!

Clash Of The Titans

95. Clash Of The Titans

In a battle between the Wither and the Enderdragon, the Wither will win most of the time.

The Walking Dead...Villager

96. An Apple A Day Keeps The Zombie Villager Away

You can turn a zombie villager back into a villager by first splashing them with a potion of weakness, then feeding them a regular golden apple. If you are successful, the zombie will hiss and start to shudder. In a few minutes, the zombie will turn into a villager. Works only with zombie villagers, not regular zombies. If you are curing many zombie villagers at once, keep them separated so the uncured zombie villagers won't attack the cured ones.

Chicken Jockey

97. Flying Zombie

Chicken jockeys do not take fall damage, as the chicken flaps its wings quickly, slowing the falling speed.

98. Quick Chicken

The chicken moves at the speed of the baby zombie, which is much faster than a normal chicken. Chicken jockeys can also track the player over a very large distance as they run very fast.

99. Watch Out For Junior!

Chicken jockeys can pick up/equip items.

100. Use The Seeds

Chicken jockeys won't attack players if the chicken notices him/her holding seeds, and will follow like a normal chicken.

101. Waterproof

Chicken jockeys will not hurt a player in water.

My Bodyguard

102. Nothing Can Get Me Down

Iron golems and snow golems take no fall damage.

103. Loyal Till The End

Iron Golems will never harm their maker.

104. Unlimited Snow

You can get unlimited snow from a trapped Snow Golem.

105. Rain, Rain Go Away

Snow Golems are harmed by rain.

Guardians Of The Ocean Galaxy

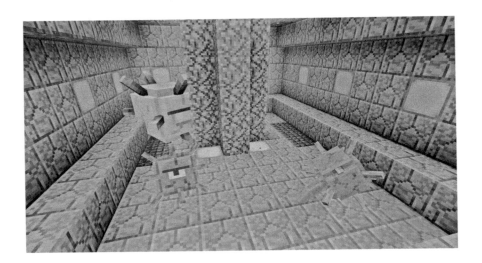

106. Surf and Turf

Regular Guardians spawn in ocean monuments.

107. A Fish With A Laser Beam?!!

Regular Guardians attack squid and players with a web/beam.

108. Pick Up The Pieces

Regular Guardians drop Prismarine shards, Prismarine crystals and raw fish when you kill them.

109. The Godfather

An Elder Guardian is a boss-like variant of Guardians.

110. Three Times The Trouble

There are 3 Elder Guardians in each ocean monument.

111. Getting Tired?

Elder Guardians inflict Mining Fatigue III on the player for 5 minutes.

112. Pick Up That Sponge

Elder Guardians drop a wet sponge when killed.

The Mob Circus

113. Baby Mobs Egg

If you right click a mob with a spawn egg, it will spawn a baby mob.

114. Naming a Mob

Naming a mob with a nametag or putting the spawn egg in an anvil and renaming it will cause the creature to never despawn.

115. Mob Unfriendly Biomes

Hostile mobs don't spawn in mushroom islands, just behind them, jungles are one of the safest places to be at night.

116. Mobs and Vines

Zombies can climb vines so watch out!

Trading Up

117. More Power Trading

Villagers can trade up, offering more trades per level.

118. Rotten Meat For Sale

Priests will buy rotten meat, and trade for valuable items like emeralds; so collect as much Zombie meat as you can. Then trade emeralds to buy more useful items.

119. Coal, Not Just For Burning

Weaponsmiths and Toolsmiths trade coal for emeralds, then you can use emeralds to buy more useful items.

120. Enchanted Trading

The Armorer and Weaponsmith villagers (black apron) sell enchanted weapons.

121. Saving The Best For Last

You can trade for Eye of Ender From Cleric Priests (Purple Robe), after you make a few trades with him.

122. Trade Your Way To The Finish Line

Instead of mining for most of your items, you can spend your time trading with villagers and get many of the items you need to complete your Minecraft quest.

Man's Best Friend

123. Zombie Jerky

Dogs/wolves don't get poisoned by rotten flesh. Feed Dogs/wolves rotten flesh and they won't get the hunger status effect either.

124. Which Direction Is It Pointing?

The direction a dog's tail is pointing will tell you it's level of health. It's at its highest strength when it is pointing sideways.

Meow!

125. Cats Always Land On Their Feet

Ocelots take no fall damage.

126. Scaredy Cat

Creepers are afraid of Cats.

Colored Baby Sheep

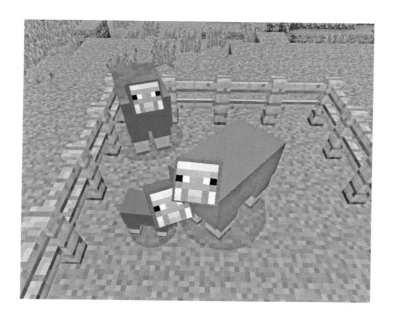

127. Colored Baby Sheep

If you breed two sheep of different color together you will get a new baby sheep with the combined color of the two parents.

128. Colored Wool

If you dye a sheep and shear it, you will get wool the color of the dyed sheep. Saves time dying wool.

Cowboy Pigs

129. Giddyup Piggy!

Pigs can be ridden, you just need a saddle, which you can find in treasure chests in dungeons. Place the saddle on a pig, climb on with a right click, and you can go anywhere the pig wants to take you.

130. Take Control Of That Pig

To control your pig while riding it, attach a carrot to a fishing rod to create a carrot-on-a-stick. Right-click for a speed boost!

131. Pig Climbing

When riding pigs, they can climb ladders and vines.

The Most Important Meal Of The Day

132. Rabbit Stew, Yum!

Cooked Rabbit Meat can be combined with a Baked Potato, a Carrot, a Mushroom (either color) and a Bowl to make Rabbit Stew, which is the most filling food in the game.

Fill Up Your Saddle Bags

133. Traveling Chest

You can put a chest on donkeys and mules to carry your things around.

Taming And Breeding Magic

134. Breeding Sheep

To make two sheep breed you have to give them wheat. Give it to them both, and then a little baby sheep comes out.

135. Breeding Cows

To make cows breed, give them some wheat.

136. Breeding Mooshroom

To make a baby Mooshroom, give Mooshroom wheat. The baby Mooshroom does not have any mushrooms on its back like the older ones do.

But, if you shear the Mooshroom parents, the baby Mooshroom will no longer follow them.

137. Breeding Cats

To make Cats breed, give them raw fish.

138. Breeding Pigs

To make pigs breed, give them some carrots, and then a little baby pig will be born.

139. Breeding Chickens

To make chickens breed, give them some seeds. Nether Wart works too.

140. Breeding Wolves/Dogs

To make wolves breed, you first have to tame them by giving both of them bones. Then you could give them any cooked meat, like steak. Make sure they are standing up. After that, they will breed a little baby wolf.

141. Breeding Rabbits

Rabbits can be tamed and bred using carrots, golden carrots or dandelions.

142. Like Momma Like Baby

Breeding tamed animals makes the baby tamed as well.

143. Where'd My Mommy Go?

All bred animals follow their parents.

Remote Control

144. Use a Bow and Arrow To Activate Pressure Plates

The Bow and Arrow can activate a wooden pressure plate, even if it hits on the side of a block. You can use this trick to turn on Redstone Lamp, trigger traps in the distance, or open doors.

Shoot Fireworks...Sideways!

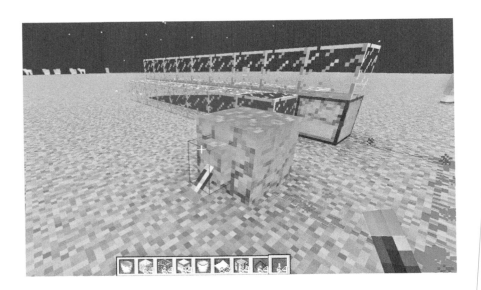

145. Shoot Fireworks...Sideways

You can direct fireworks sideways by placing a dispenser in a constructed glass tube around the dispenser, then adding water to the tube. Activate the dispensers and you can shoot your fireworks sideways.

146. Create An Army Tank

Add a pressure plate to the Fireworks Sideways Dispenser and some tank decorations and you can build a working tank.

Stained Glass

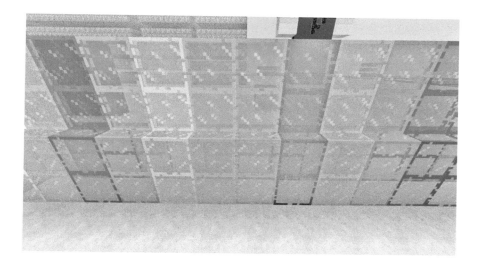

147. Stained Glass

Stained Glass can be made by crafting glass with any available Dye. You can create some beautiful designs with it.

H20 Magic

148. Floating Water

If ice has no solid block underneath it, nothing will happen when you break it. If ice has a solid block underneath it, it'll turn into water. If you break the ice and then break the block under it, the water will float in mid-air.

149. Invisible Ice

You can't see ice through water or vice versa

Infinite Water

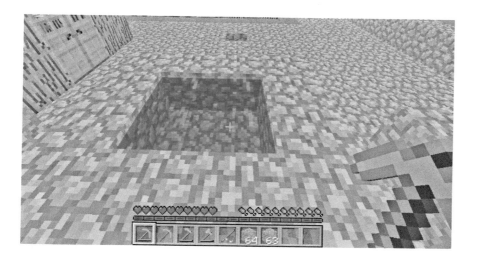

150. Infinite Water

You can create a pool of water that can be infinitely used by putting two water sources in two corners of a 2X2 block square and taking water from each of the corners.

Easier Obsidian

151. Get Obsidian Without Mining

Don't mine obsidian to make a nether portal, placing lava in a mold and pouring water over it is much faster. Use an infinite water source next to a lava to do it.

152. Easy Mining

If you spawn a Wither, and trap it in a cave made of obsidian, and attack it, it will mine the obsidian for you.

Mob Sand

153. Fireproof Mobs

Mobs that stand on Soul Sand do not burn in daylight.

154. Slow Sand

Using ice under soul sand makes mobs move even slower.

Bouncy Blocks

155. Bouncy Blocks

Slime Blocks are crafted from Slime Balls. Slime blocks are bouncy: you can fall on them from any height and instead of taking damage you will bounce.

156. Reduce The Bounce

Holding down the jump key as you land on a slime block will reduce the height of your bounce.

Going Sailing?

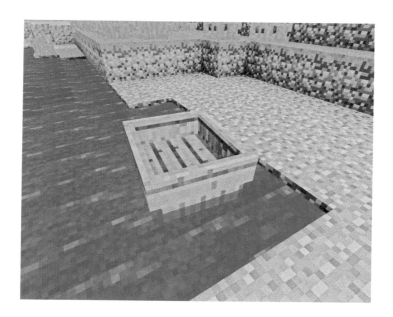

157. Need A Little Push?

If you're going on a ride in a boat push the boat out before hopping in. This gives your boat a little speed boost.

158. Protect Your Boat

You can line your boat dock with wool or soul sand, and even if your boat bumps into it at full speed, it won't break.

159. Lily Pad Mines

Your boat breaks after hitting 3 lily pads, so avoid them in swamps.

Regular Or Unleaded?

160. Lava Fuel

Use a lava bucket to fuel a furnace and cook 100 items in a furnace.

161. Blaze Rod Fuel

A blaze rod can fuel a furnace and can cook 12 items in a furnace as well.

162. Furniture Fuel

Furnaces can be fuelled by almost any item made of wood such as saplings, jukeboxes, bookshelves, fences, trapdoors, crafting tables, mushroom blocks and chests.

What Time Is It?

163. In a cave you can tell if its day or night by the color of the fog. Grey fog means its day, dark fog means it is night.

164. You can get rid of cave fog completely by creating holes in the cave that lead to the surface.

Nuclear Bomb

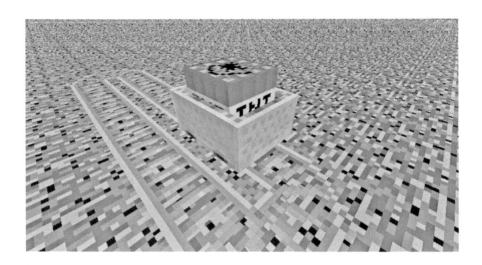

165. Create The Nuclear Bomb Effect

If you summon multiple TNT minecarts on each other, by using the summon command, they will have the nuclear bomb effect when detonated.

166. Minecart Launcher

Also, if you are nearby, it will launch you hundreds of feet into the air. If you are in survival mode, say your goodbyes.

Secret Paintings

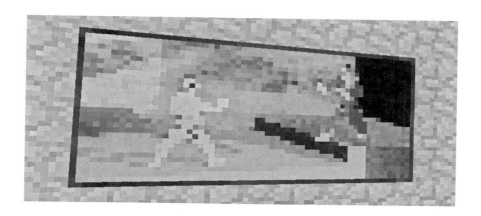

167. Walk Through Paintings

You can place paintings on signs, doors, and a lot of other things you can walk through, making an excellent door for a secret room that you enter from a painting room.

You Need Your Sleep!

168. Sleep Under Water

You can place beds underwater and sleep in them. But be prepared to wake up soaked! To put a bed under water, first make a hole, add the bed, then fill it with water.

169. Sleep Under Lava

You can also place beds under lava and sleep in them. But, be prepared to wake up on fire! To put a bed under lava, first make a hole, add the bed, then fill it with lava.

170. Bed Bomb

If you try to sleep in a bed in the Nether or the End it will explode. Ouch!

171. Control The Weather

You can sleep in the daytime if there is a thunderstorm going on. Waking up causes the rain to stop.

Round Trip Teleport

172. Chest Teleport

If you want to get one item in a chest far away (even in a PVP zone), just toss an Ender Pearl there, then toss one straight up right before the other one hits the ground. You'll teleport to the chest, grab your stuff quickly, and you will automatically be teleported back.

Pour That Energy Drink On Your Head

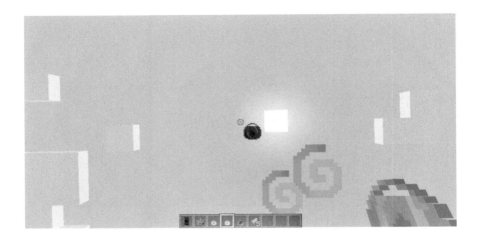

173. Maximum Potion Effects

You can get the maximum effect of a potion by throwing it in the sky and having it land on your body or by launching it at yourself through a dispenser.

Conclusion

We hope that you've learned enough secrets, tips, tricks and hints that will allow you to go out and have even more fun in the world of Minecraft. Or hopefully you've learned just enough to make you dangerous (or just impress your friends).

We appreciate you buying this book and if you did find some useful and interesting tips, your positive review on Amazon would be greatly appreciated.

Thank You,
The Minecraft Guys at Herobrine Books

CPSIA information can be obtained
at www.ICGtesting.com
Printed in the USA
LVOW01s1538031215
465066LV00001B/1/P